T0349147

FIND YOUR POWER

CRYSTALS

An Hachette UK Company
www.hachette.co.uk

First published in Great Britain in 2023 by Godsfield,
an imprint of Octopus Publishing Group Ltd
Carmelite House, 50 Victoria Embankment, London EC4Y 0DZ
www.octopusbooks.co.uk

ISBN 978-1-8418-1551-0

A CIP catalogue record for this book is available from the British Library

Printed and bound in China

10 9 8 7 6 5 4 3 2 1

Publisher: Lucy Pessell
Designer: Isobel Platt
Editor: Feyi Oyesanya
Assistant Editor: Samina Rahman
Production Controller: Allison Gonsalves

FIND YOUR POWER

CRYSTALS

TESSA SALE

GODSFIELD

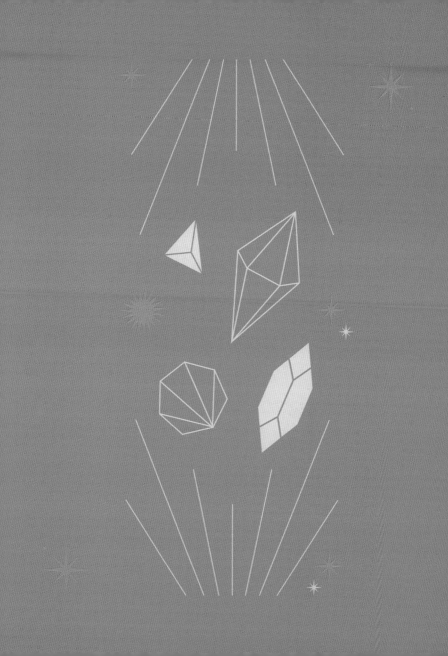

CONTENTS

FIND
YOUR
POWER

When daily life becomes busy and your time and energy is pulled in many different directions, it can be difficult to find time to nourish yourself. Prioritizing your own wellbeing can be a struggle and you risk feeling overwhelmed, unsure of where to turn and what you need in order to feel lighter and find your inner strength.

Taking some time to focus on yourself, answering questions you may be avoiding or facing problems that are simmering away under the surface is the best gift you can give yourself. But it can be difficult to know where to start.

Sometimes all you need to learn life's big lessons is a little guidance. In this series of books you will learn about personal healing, self-empowerment and how to nourish your spirit. Explore practices which will help you to get clear on what you really want, and that will encourage you to acknowledge – and deal with – any limiting beliefs or negative thoughts that might be holding you back in living life to your fullest power.

These books provide invaluable advice on how to create the best conditions for a healthier, happier, and more fulfilled life. Bursting with essential background, revealing insights and useful activities and exercises to enable you to understand and expand your personal practices every day, it's time to delve into your spiritual journey and truly Find Your Power.

Other titles in the series:

- *Find Your Power: Tarot*
- *Find Your Power: Manifest*
- *Find Your Power: Numerology*
- *Find Your Power: Runes*
- *Find Your Power: Mindfulness*
- *Find Your Power: Chakra*
- *Find Your Power: Meditation*

INTRODUCTION

Beautiful and mysterious, crystals have been used for thousands of years for decoration, protection and healing. Archaeologists have discovered beads, carvings and jewellery made of amber, jet, turquoise, lapis, garnet, quartz and other crystals in excavations in every part of the world. Ancient people valued crystals for their magical and spiritual powers. Rulers wore rings and crowns set with precious gems. Shamans and healers used crystal amulets and gemstone remedies for healing and protection.

Crystals gain their power from the way they are created. The ancient belief that crystals are the bones of Mother Earth is not far from scientific truth. Millions of years ago, superheated gases and mineral solutions were forced upwards from the Earth's core towards the surface. As the molten rock gradually cooled, the mineral molecules formed orderly patterns.

The appearance of a crystal is affected by its mineral content, the temperature and pressure at which it's formed and its rate of cooling.

Hard and transparent crystals like diamonds were formed under immense heat and pressure. Softer stones such as calcite were created at lower temperatures.

Today we understand that the helpful properties of crystals arise from their structure. They have lattice-like structures at a molecular level, which gives crystals their unique ability to absorb, store, generate and transmit energy.

As you'll discover in this book, this ability allows crystals to be used to amplify, direct and balance the flow of life-force in your body and surroundings. You'll find that working with crystals is a gentle and natural way to improve your physical, emotional and spiritual wellbeing.

WORKING WITH CRYSTAL ENERGY

If you are just beginning to work with crystals, this chapter provides basic information about choosing, cleansing and energizing your crystals. If you do not own any crystals, to get started you'll need a piece of quartz with a natural point and a few round or oval crystals about the size of a walnut. A good first buy might include a clear quartz point and small tumbled pieces of amethyst, blue lace agate, rose quartz, tiger's eye and red jasper. If you already have a collection of personal crystals, you'll find helpful tips in this chapter about preparing your crystals for practical use.

Crystals can be grouped in a number of ways, but the most useful qualities for practical purposes are a crystal's hardness, shape and colour.

As you might expect, the diamond is one of the hardest, while talc, which easily breaks up into common talcum powder, is one of the softest. Organic gemstones such as amber, coral and jet are also quite fragile; whilst quartz, amethyst and gemstones such as emerald, sapphire and ruby are quite strong.

Hardness is important when choosing crystals for healing and other practical purposes. Softer crystals can be used to absorb negative physical and emotional energy. It is the harder crystals that make the best choices for jewellery.

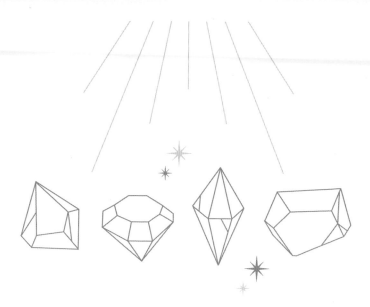

In their natural form, many crystals are rough, sharp or jagged – more like stones than translucent gems.

Many of the small stones in crystal shops have been tumbled, a process that polishes a stone to enhance its colour and beauty. Polishing alters their appearance but doesn't affect its useful properties. A crystal's shape influences how it transmits energy.

Single point crystals, focus energy in a straight line. In general, pointed crystals are used to transmit

energy or draw it off, depending on which way the point is facing. A symmetrical crystal wand is likely to have been artificially shaped.

In their natural form, many crystals are rough, sharp or jagged.

Double-terminated crystals have a point on each end. Because they send and receive energy simultaneously, they are useful for balancing and integrating opposing forces, such as breaking up old patterns and overcoming addictions.

Crystal clusters radiate the energy of the crystal to the surrounding environment. They are useful for cleansing the energy in a room.

And lastly, geodes have a cave-like interior that holds and amplifies energy, releasing it slowly to their surroundings. They are a good choice for bedrooms, where a soothing flow of soft energy is beneficial.

A crystal's shape influences how it transmits energy.

**A crystal's colour
energy can
be drawn into
your body's
energy field.**

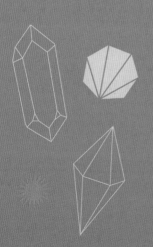

The most important quality for crystal healing is its colour. As you may know, white light is really a mixture of colours, called a spectrum. A glass prism: a crystal drop hanging in a window or the rainbow created by raindrops on a sunny day, reveals that the seven colours of the spectrum are red, orange, yellow, green, blue, indigo and violet.

You will already have experienced how colours affect your emotions. Wearing a bright yellow sweater can make you feel happy, while sitting in a room with cool blue walls can be soothing and relaxing.

In colour therapy, the body is bathed in coloured light, or coloured crystals are placed directly on the body. Because of the links between the seven colours of the spectrum and your body's life-force (see pages 22-25), a crystal's colour energy can be drawn into your body's energy field through your optic nerve or, as some believe, directly through your skin, diffusing or absorbing energy as needed for a healthy balance.

Though you can certainly choose crystals for the colours that attract you most, here are some of the traditional meanings of crystal colours:

- **Red crystals:** such as red jasper and bloodstone, increase your power, passion, courage and physical energy.

- **Orange crystals:** such as carnelian, fire opal enhance self-esteem, confidence and creativity.

- **Green crystals:** such as green fluorite and green aventurine soothe the emotions and promote harmony and balance.

- **White or clear crystals:** such as clear quartz and moonstone promote new beginnings, peace and tranquillity.

HOW CRYSTALS WORK

Crystals have a subtle but measurable 'vibration' or electromagnetic field, as does every object, including your body. The regularity of a crystal's structure makes this vibration especially consistent and helps crystals to diffuse valuable energy and absorb negative energy as needed to preserve a healthy balance.

Additionally, it may be that the 'good vibes' you get from placing a stunning geode or crystal cluster on your desk are due both to the crystal's energy field *and* to your own positive emotional response to its radiant colour, striking shape and natural beauty.

Crystal healing may work in a similar way. Many of the healing techniques you'll find in this book ask you to pay attention to how you are feeling and then to take some action to relieve any problems, such as placing crystals in particular positions on your body or bathing in a gem essence. Paying attention to your body and emotions is always the first step to healing. In some cases, a crystal's vibration may simply help you to focus your own potent healing energy on what hurts.

Traditional wisdom has linked crystals to particular parts of the body for thousands of years. Some of these texts are based on the links between a crystal's colour and vibration and the body's subtle energy system (see pages 19-25).

Eastern traditions such as yoga, Buddhism and Hinduism teach that in addition to a physical body, you have an energy body. Balancing the flow of life energy through the channels and the centres of your energy body is said to improve your physical and emotional health and your spiritual wellbeing.

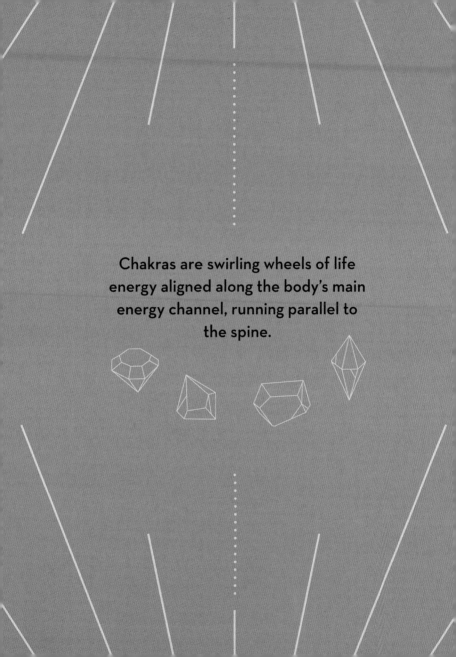

Chakras are swirling wheels of life energy aligned along the body's main energy channel, running parallel to the spine.

CRYSTALS AND THE CHAKRAS

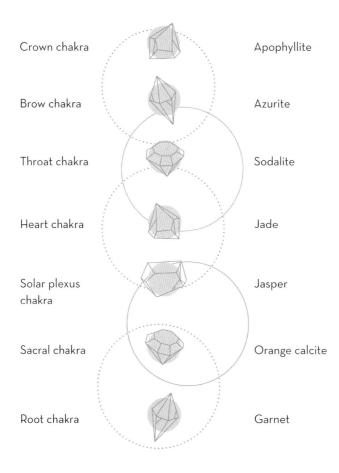

Crown chakra — Apophyllite

Brow chakra — Azurite

Throat chakra — Sodalite

Heart chakra — Jade

Solar plexus chakra — Jasper

Sacral chakra — Orange calcite

Root chakra — Garnet

Energy healing, which includes crystal therapy, is based on the idea that you can regulate your life energy by bringing attention to the body's seven energy centres, called the chakras. The chakras are swirling wheels of life energy aligned along the body's main energy channel, running parallel to the spine. Each chakra vibrates at a particular colour frequency and influences a particular set of physical, emotional and spiritual concerns.

Many of the techniques in this book are based on pairing crystals with the chakras. The next few pages detail the location of the chakras and the life issues and potential problems associated with each. You'll find the body parts influenced by each chakra and the potential health problems related to each on page 40. Studying these aids can help you determine which of the crystal techniques in this book best targets your concerns.

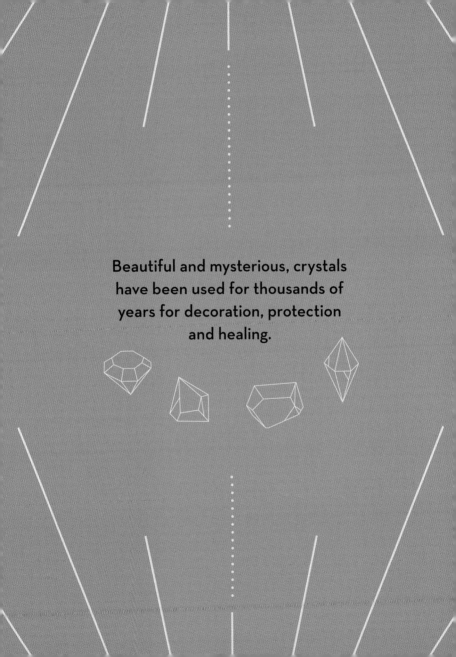

Beautiful and mysterious, crystals
have been used for thousands of
years for decoration, protection
and healing.

Each chakra vibrates at a particular colour frequency.

Chakra: Root/red

This chakra vibrating at the right frequency, can provide safety and security, stability and grounding, the ability to stand up for yourself, good judgement and self-worth.

The potential problems that could arise when it's not vibrating at the right frequency are: depression, feeling spacey and ungrounded, a lack of self-confidence, low self-esteem, risk-taking, as well as fears and phobias.

Chakra: Sacral/orange

Vibrating at the right frequency brings: flexibility, the ability to enjoy sexual pleasure and the ability to generate new ideas.

The problems that may arise at the wrong frequency can be: a lack of desire and sexual satisfaction, fear of touch and intimacy, self-neglect, blocked creativity and shame.

Chakra: Solar plexus/yellow

At the right frequency, this brings trust, power, prosperity, drive, ambition and taking responsibility for making decisions.

The wrong frequency can bring fatigue, lack of ambition, anger, a tendency to blame others, resentment and guilt.

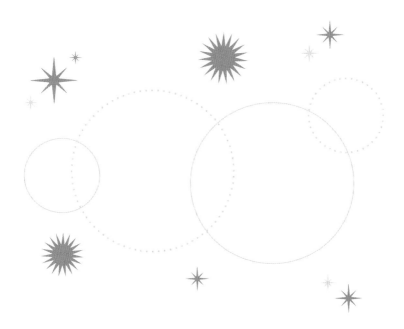

Chakra: Heart/green or pink

This chakra vibrating at the right frequency brings the ability to love and be loved, empathy, acceptance and forgiveness, and compassion.

At the wrong frequency this can bring: loneliness, self-centredness, passive-aggressiveness, bitterness and co-dependence.

Chakra: Throat/blue

At the right frequency, this chakra allows for personal expression, the ability to speak and to listen, integrity, creative and artistic self-expression, wit and humour.

At the wrong frequency, it invites: poor communication skills, unwillingness to listen, the inability to express creative ideas and lying.

Chakra: Brow/indigo

At the right frequency brings inspiration, intuition, intelligence, memory, vision, insight and wisdom.

At the wrong frequency it can lead to lack of clarity, lack of perception, unwillingness to see the truth and the inability to learn from experience.

Chakra: Crown/violet or white

At the right frequency, faith, inspiration, spirituality, values and ethics, selflessness, devotion, mystical understanding, and enlightenment, are all welcomed in.

At the wrong frequency this can invite confusion, arrogance, spiritual doubt and lack of compassion.

Crystals are excellent energy transmitters.

The right crystals for you will draw
your attention or your eye and ask to
become part of your life.

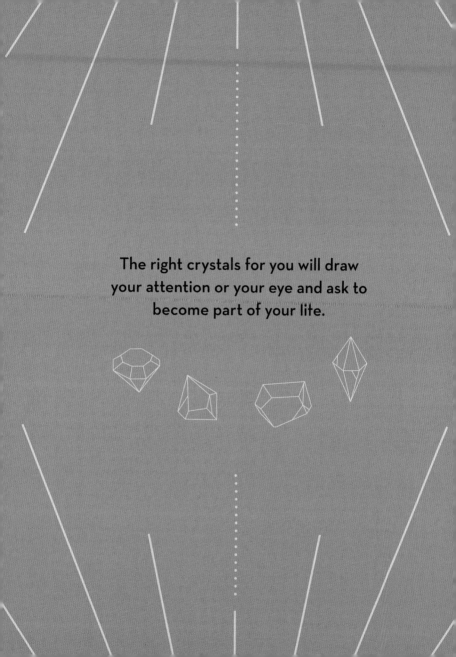

CHOOSING AND CARING FOR YOUR CRYSTAL

Though this book will suggest particular crystals, choosing crystals should be personal and intuitive. You will find that crystals have different voices and different personalities. The right crystals for you will draw your attention or your eye and ask to become part of your life.

Pick up a crystal that attracts you and hold it in your hands. Look at it from all angles and feel its weight, texture and shape. Tune in to the way the crystal feels in your hand. Close your eyes for a moment and see what you experience. You may feel a tingling on your skin or a sensation of warmth or coolness. You may also feel an energetic charge in some part of your body, such as the top of your head or the middle of your chest.

> **Crystals are like your smart and treasured friends, so treat them with respect.**

If these sensations are pleasurable, the crystal you are holding is resonating with some aspect of your body and mind, and is likely to be a good one for you to work with. If the sensation is unpleasant, it may be worthwhile reading about the crystal's properties and asking yourself whether it is bringing up something you are avoiding. Make a note of what you discover so that you can come back to this crystal later.

Once you have chosen your crystals, look after them carefully. Crystals are like your smart and treasured friends, so treat them with respect. Softer crystals and crystals with unusual shapes, such as points and clusters, can be fragile. To keep them safe, wrap each one separately in a silk scarf. Alternately, find the right place in your home or office for each crystal, such as on your desk, on your bedside table or added alongside your houseplants, near your favourite chair.

Though harder natural stones can scratch softer ones when they are stored together in a pouch, tumbled stones are in general more resistant to damage. It's perfectly fine to keep a collection of small tumbled stones in a silk bag or pouch.

Crystals that are used for healing or to balance the energy in your surroundings should be cleansed regularly. Cleansing your crystals when you first bring them home makes them uniquely yours. Cleansing them after each use rids them of negative energy and makes them ready to use again.

Some delicate crystals such as celestite or selenite can separate in water. Salt can damage other crystals, such as opals, changing their colour or making them appear dull or cloudy. If you are unsure about which cleansing method is best to use for a particular crystal, ask a knowledgeable dealer or choose one of the all-purpose methods over the page.

After you have cleansed a crystal for the first time, you can energize it for its particular task. Hold it in your hands and concentrate on the purpose for which you wish to use it. For instance, say to yourself or out loud, 'I dedicate this crystal to healing' or 'I dedicate this crystal to bringing more love into my life.' If you are not sure how you will use a crystal, you can dedicate it to a general positive purpose such as 'the highest good for all'. You may wish to repeat this process several times with a new crystal.

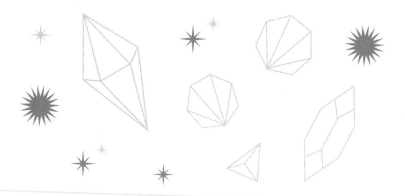

Methods of cleansing

Water and salt water: hold a crystal that can be cleansed with water under a running tap, bathe it in water mixed with salt or immerse it in a natural water source such as a stream, or a lake. As the water flows over your crystal, hold the intention that all negative energy is being washed away and the crystal is being re-energized.

Smudging: all crystals can be cleansed by being surrounded by the smoke from a sage smudge stick. This method is especially useful for large crystals or for cleansing several crystals at once.

Moonlight: all crystals can also be cleansed by bathing them in the light of the moon for a few hours. Place a crystal on your windowsill or in your garden and allow the moonlight to draw off any impurities in order to recharge the crystal's energy.

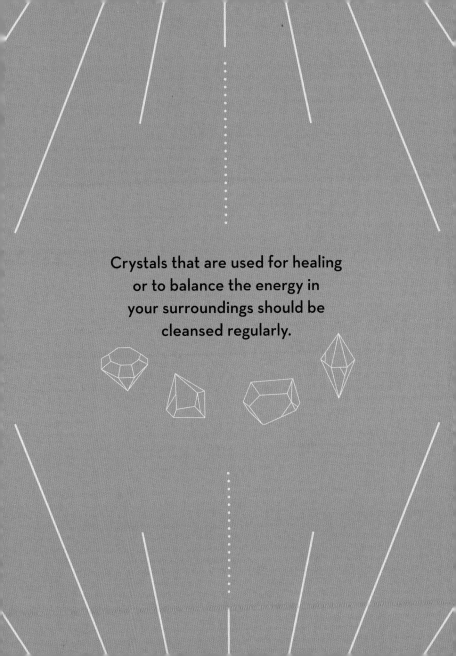

Crystals that are used for healing
or to balance the energy in
your surroundings should be
cleansed regularly.

Once ready, many of the crystal exercises involve placing crystals on your chakra points or around your body.

You'll find these most helpful when you are relaxed and uninterrupted, so close the door to your room, turn off your mobile phone and give yourself permission to focus solely on yourself.

Prepare a place where you will be comfortable lying on the floor, on a yoga mat or a folded blanket.

Larger crystals are a natural way to bring balance and beauty into your home or office. Place crystals in any room where you spend time, such as the bedroom, office or lounge. Be sure to keep these display crystals clean by dusting them regularly using a soft cloth or feather duster.

To keep your energy continuous, wearing or carrying crystal jewellery, such as pendants, rings or earrings is a useful way to do so. You can also just carry the crystal you are working with in a small silk pouch in your pocket or bag.

Another way to draw energy from crystals, is to create a gem essence. Gem essences have a subtle and gentle healing effect. They can be rubbed on an affected part of your body, poured into your bathwater or put into an atomizer bottle and sprayed around a room.

How to prepare a simple gem essence:

1. Place a cleansed crystal that can be immersed in water in a clean glass bowl filled with spring water. (If the crystal should not be immersed in water, place it in a small glass bowl and place the small bowl in a larger water-filled bowl.)

2. Place the bowl where it can stand in the sunlight for several hours.

3. Remove the crystal and pour the essence into a glass bottle with an airtight stopper. To keep an essence for more than a week, double the volume of the liquid in the bottle by adding clear alcohol or vodka as a preservative.

4. Label your essences with the crystal's name and the date of preparation. Store them in a cool, dark place.

Gem essences have a subtle and gentle healing effect.

CRYSTALS FOR WELLBEING

Healing yourself is a uniquely personal process. The first step is awareness. You train yourself to listen to the messages your body is sending and use your intuition to figure out what your body needs. Sometimes, although what you are experiencing is a physical symptom like a headache or a digestive upset, the underlying cause may be a combination of physical, emotional and even spiritual factors. Working with crystals gives you the opportunity to tune into what's happening at all of these levels and to stimulate your body's natural ability to heal.

Though healing with crystals feels very modern, the practice is actually very old. The earliest records of crystal healing come from ancient Egypt.

The theory behind crystal healing is simple. In addition to its physical parts, your body has an energy system. Traditional healing methods focus on regulating the flow of energy through the chakras and channels that link every part of your anatomy. You can readily experience the effects

Crystal healing is not a substitute for traditional medical care, but it can help in many practical ways.

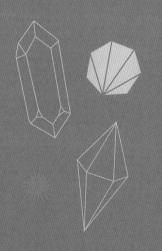

of this energy flow. On days of high energy, you find it easy to get things done, but when your energy is blocked, you may feel tired or confused.

When you are ill, some aspect of your body's energy is out of

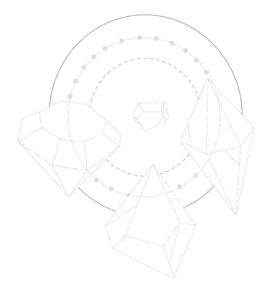

balance. Illness may be your body calling your attention to a life issue you have ignored for too long. Focusing your awareness on your condition encourages you to make better lifestyle choices and address both your symptoms and their underlying causes.

Crystals are excellent energy transmitters. Their crystalline structure amplifies your healing intentions and restores and rebalances your body's energy by removing blockages, drawing off excess energy and shoring up weaknesses. Crystal healing is not a substitute for traditional medical care, but it can help in many practical ways. Healing with crystals also empowers you to take personal responsibility for your health, using simple, natural methods.

The crystal healing outline on page 40 shows that the link between a specific crystal and a health problem is often based on the crystal's colour and frequency of vibration or subtle electromagnetic field. Crystals with a lower vibration (red, orange and yellow crystals) heal conditions related to the lower chakras, while crystals with a higher vibration (green, blue, indigo and violet crystals) work best on conditions of the upper chakras.

You'll find different ways throughout this chapter for using healing crystals, but this outline

Healing yourself is a uniquely personal process. The first step is awareness.

can help you to choose the right crystal quickly and easily.

To use crystal energy to support or relieve a particular condition that's directly linked to a chakra, place one of the listed crystals on the chakra and leave it in place for 20 minutes while you relax quietly.

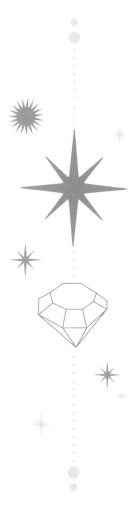

When you are
ill, some aspect
of your body's
energy is out of
balance.

On days of high energy, you find it easy to get things done, but when your energy is blocked, you may feel tired or confused.

CRYSTAL HEALING OUTLINE

The root chakra, can be associated with problems such as haemorrhoids, problems with hips, knees etc. Helpful crystals are smoky quarts, garnet, bloodstone, ruby and jasper.

The sacral chakra, is said to be linked to problems such as lower back pain, and bladder infections. Crystals that you can use to help, are carnelian, orange calcite, citrine, moonstone and fire opal.

The solar plexus chakra, can have physical problems such as ulcers, indigestion, and gallstones. Helpful crystals are amber, golden topaz, sunstone, yellow jasper, and yellow calcite.

The heart chakra, can be associated with problems such as high blood pressure, bronchitis, and asthma. Helpful crystals are rose quartz, pink tourmaline, pink danburite, green citrine and jade.

The throat chakra, can have physical problems such as laryngitis, sore throat, and frequent colds. Helpful crystals are turquoise, aquamarine, blue lace gate, celestite, and blue sapphire.

The brow chakra, can have problems such as epilepsy, eye problems and sinus infections. Helpful crystals are amethyst, electric blue obsidian, blue chalcedony, iolite, and azurite.

The crown chakra, relates to problems such as epilepsy, eye problems and sinus infections. Helpful crystals are amethyst, electric blue obsidian, blue chalcedony, iolite, and azurite.

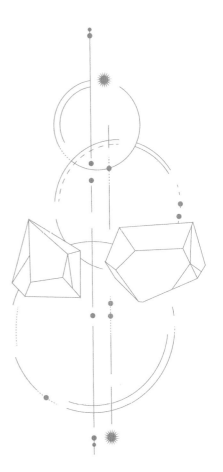

PAIN
RELIEF

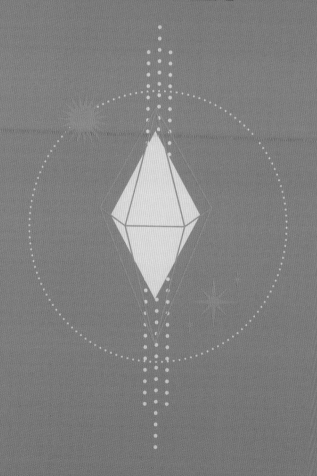

Pain anywhere in your body is a message that something is wrong. The discomfort may be due to a physical illness or it may reflect emotional or spiritual distress. Crystal healing is most effective when you take the time to investigate all possible reasons for your discomfort, keeping in mind that the cause may be a combination of factors.

If you have frequent headaches, for example, start by consulting the crystal healing outline on page 40. As it shows, headaches are related to the brow chakra and may result from physical problems with your eyes or your sinuses.

You'll also want to consult the chakra plan on pages 22-25, which lists some life issues influenced by the brow chakra. Ask yourself: What am I unclear about? Exploring these questions empowers your crystal healing and encourages you to make lifestyle changes to avoid the problem in the future.

Quartz is the most effective and versatile crystal pain-reliever. In Chinese medicine, clear quartz is considered to contain the pure essence of chi or life-force.

Because it can affect every chakra, a quartz crystal can be used to relieve any kind of pain. Smoky quartz crystals melt away energy blockages, and draw off and absorb the excess of blocked energy that may be contributing to the pain or discomfort. Clear quartz crystals release their concentrated natural life-force energy to revitalize and restore balance.

QUARTZ PAIN RELIEF

For this technique you will need one smoky quartz crystal with a single termination point and one clear quartz crystal with a single termination point. Lie down on a yoga mat or folded blanket or sit comfortably on the floor.

1. Hold the smoky quartz crystal in your left hand with the termination pointing away from the painful area. Move the crystal in a small circle just above the painful area in an anticlockwise motion. As you circle the crystal, breathe into the painful area, carrying with your breath the intention to release the pain. Imagine the crystal is a sponge drawing off and absorbing any painful or blocked energy.

2. When the pain has decreased, switch hands and crystals. Hold the clear quartz crystal in your right hand with the termination pointing towards the area being healed. Move the crystal in a small circle just above the area in a clockwise motion. As you circle the crystal, imagine that the crystal is releasing natural life-force energy to revitalize and restore your body's optimum energy balance.

3. Be sure to wash your hands and cleanse the crystals after use.

Crystal healing is most effective when you take the time to investigate all possible reasons for your discomfort.

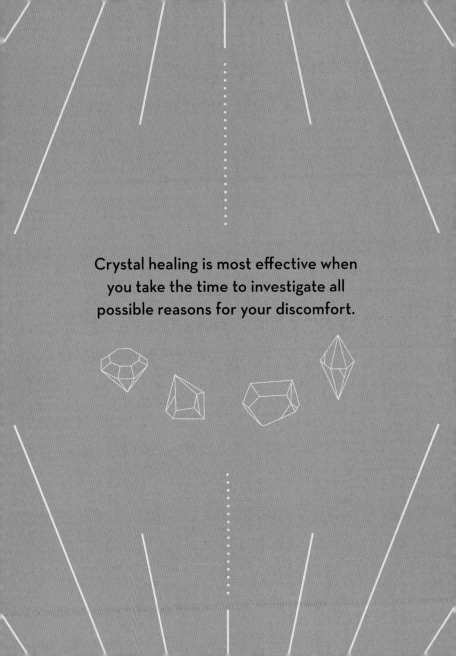

LISTEN TO THE MESSAGES

As with any crystal healing technique, paying attention to the messages your symptoms may be communicating can make your self-healing more effective. Unrelieved tension and stress and unhealthy lifestyle habits can weaken your immune system and make you more vulnerable to catching a cold or flu virus. Ask yourself: What are the sources of stress in my life and what can I do to minimize them? Am I getting enough rest and exercise? Is my diet healthy?

You'll find crystal healing techniques for strengthening your immune system and relieving your tension and stress later in this book (see pages 53, and 69-73).

As you have learned, the throat chakra, which influences the throat, neck and mouth, vibrates at the frequency of blue light. So the best crystal for problems affecting your throat, such as a sore throat, laryngitis, swollen glands or hoarseness due to a cold or flu, is blue lace agate. This lovely powdery or periwinkle blue stone, often banded with white lacy threads, harmonizes perfectly with the energy of the throat chakra, activating it to help soothe and calm a painful throat. To do so, you can create gem essence-infused water, and gargle every two hours if needed.

Wearing jewellery made with blue lace agate is both decorative, and also healing for your throat.

A cabochon is a gemstone that has been shaped and polished. The resulting stone usually has a convex top and a flat back. When it is banded with sterling silver, it makes

Paying attention to the messages your symptoms may be communicating can make your self-healing more effective.

a beautiful pendant that can be worn on a chain around your neck. To strengthen the energy of your throat chakra and protect against frequent sore throats, wear a blue lace agate cabochon pendant on a 35 cm (14 in) silver chain, with the flat back of the stone resting against the bare skin at the base of your neck.

Small blue lace agate beads, ranging in size from 5–8 mm (¼–¾ in), can also be strung into a lariat necklace that can be wrapped loosely several times around your neck. Sometimes smaller beads of royal blue lapis lazuli are interspersed with the agate, increasing the beauty of the necklace and its healing power.

Digestion is under the influence of the solar plexus chakra, located at the abdomen above the navel. Radiating golden-yellow fire energy, this is like an inner sun, fuelling not only digestion but also

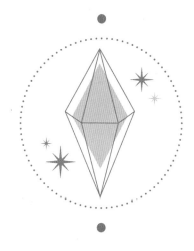

your vitality, drive and passion. When it's fully functioning, life energy shines outwards from your body's core, helping you get nourishment from both food and life experiences. When it is out of balance, you may feel irritable, angry or resentful and have a tendency to blame others when things go wrong. Not surprisingly, you may also experience stomach aches and other digestive upsets.

Citrine and other yellow crystals carry the power of the sun. Meditating with a citrine crystal can help to strengthen your solar plexus chakra, stimulating digestion, strengthening the bladder and kidneys and relieving constipation and other digestive ills.

Wearing jewellery made with blue lace agate is both decorative, and also healing for your throat.

INNER SUN MEDITATION

For this meditation, you will need one piece of citrine. A small polished stone, a point or a geode work equally well.

1. Sit comfortably cross-legged on the floor or on a chair with your feet flat on the ground. Be sure that your back is straight. Close your eyes.

2. Hold the piece of citrine with your hands resting comfortably against your abdomen.

3. Breathe slowly and deeply, taking air all the way down to your belly. As you breathe in, imagine that the citrine crystal in your hands is shining like the sun, energizing with its golden light the inner sun of your solar plexus chakra.

4. As you breathe out, imagine that the warming and invigorating energy of your inner sun is spreading throughout your body, strengthening your digestive system, healing its ills and filling you with vitality, warmth and passion.

A crystal's power will be enhanced if
you dedicate it to a specific role.

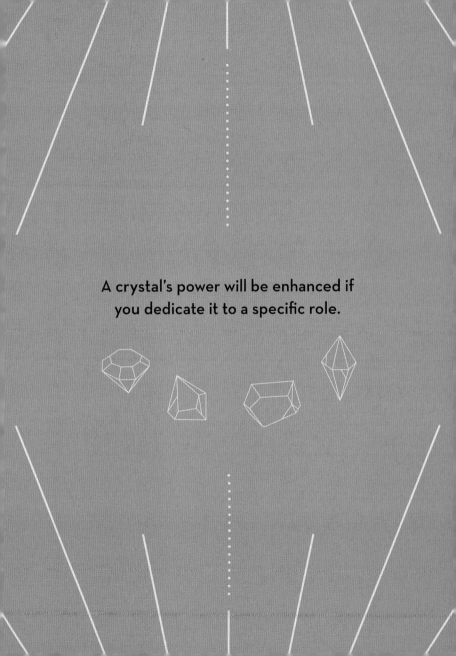

CARNELIAN ENERGY WEB

Orange-red carnelian empowers the sacral chakra, strengthening your reproductive system. It combats anxiety; reduces irritability and helps you stay calm, and cheerful, even under difficult circumstances.

For this technique you will need six clear quartz points with single terminations and a tumbled carnelian crystal.

1. Lie down on a yoga mat or folded blanket. Place a flat pillow under your head to ease any tension in your neck.

2. Place the six quartz points around your body, one above your head, one beneath your feet and two each at the level of your elbows and your knees. The terminations should point away from your body.

3. Place the carnelian crystal on your sacral chakra, situated just below your navel.

4. Relax and focus your attention on the rise and fall of your abdomen as you breathe. Remind yourself that you are confident and courageous. Leave the crystals in place for 20 minutes.

IMMUNE STIMULATOR

The immune system can also be strengthened with crystal therapy. As you have learned, quartz is a powerful master healer.

For this technique you will need one aqua aura quartz point and one clear quartz tumbled crystal.

1. Lie down on a yoga mat or folded blanket. Place a flat pillow under your head to ease any tension in your neck.

2. Place the aqua aura point on your thymus – centre of chest (breastbone) – and the tumbled clear quartz crystal on the centre of your forehead.

3. Leave the aqua aura and quartz crystals in place and remain still for 10–20 minutes.

4. Be sure to cleanse both the crystals after you have finished with them.

> **Crystal therapy can also support natural detoxification, strengthening your immune system.**

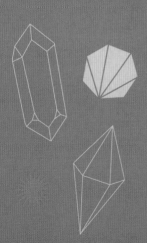

Detoxification means helping your body cleanse itself of the residues of living in the modern world, including toxins from air and water pollution, food additives, and other environmental hazards.

Eating a diet rich in fibre, including whole grains, pulses, nuts, fruits and vegetables aids the elimination of waste. Drinking plenty of water – 2 litres (3½ pints) – every day is also helpful. A great morning detox drink to assist your kidneys and liver is a glass of hot water mixed with the juice of half a lemon.

Crystal therapy can also support natural detoxification and strengthen your immune system.

The immune system can also be weakened by addictions to alcohol, food, tobacco and drugs. Addictions not only have negative physical consequences but also bring anxiety, stress, confusion and other psychological and emotional ills.

Amethyst is the most useful crystal for helping you to overcome addictions. A stone of the mind, it brings calmness and clarity, and promotes sobriety and abstinence. A famous ancient detoxifier, amethyst also helps to balance overworked, and overwhelmed mental states.

In Greek mythology, Amethyst was a mortal maiden who incurred the wrath of Dionysus, the god of wine. When she cried out to the goddess Artemis for help, Artemis protected the girl by turning her into a pillar of white quartz. When he realized what had happened, Dionysus shed tears of remorse into his wine. The goblet spilled and the wine stained the quartz purple.

Since that time, purple amethyst crystals have been used in Greece as a means of aiding sobriety. Even today, goblets carved from amethyst are said to prevent drinkers from being overcome by wine and spirits.

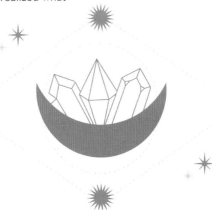

AMETHYST HEALING

Try some of the following more contemporary techniques to focus the healing power of amethyst on your addictive habits:

Wear an amethyst pendant, ring or earrings to keep the sobering power of amethyst with you during the day. When you put on the jewellery, remind yourself that you love yourself enough to overcome habits that compromise your health and peace of mind.

Place a small dish of amethyst crystals in your home or on your desk – anywhere where their vibrant purple colour can symbolize the resolutions you've made to change your behaviour.

Make an alcohol-free amethyst gem essence (see page 32 for instructions). Bottle it and splash a little on your pulse points at your wrists and the base of your neck whenever your willpower needs a boost.

Place an amethyst crystal under your pillow before you go to sleep to put yourself in touch with your feelings and values as you rest.

Jewellery made from amethyst keeps
the wearer grounded through the
trials of the day.

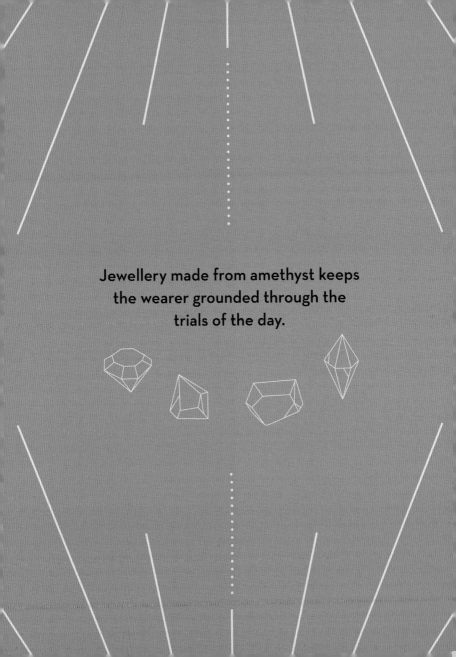

Many people have occasional difficulties falling asleep or staying asleep. Sometimes the problem is caused by stress or by practices such as drinking excessive amounts of coffee or alcohol. Working out regularly at the gym, writing in your journal or meditating can help you manage your stress so that it does not stand in the way of a good night's sleep.

Keeping a sleep diary can also help you become aware of behaviour patterns that may be disturbing your sleep.

Every day during a two-week period write down what time you go to bed, what you do before bedtime, what you eat and drink, how long you sleep and other sleep-related information. Review your entries regularly and make changes in your routine to see whether they improve your sleep.

CRYSTALS USED FOR WELLBEING

Moonstone, which is translucent white, cream or yellow-grey, with an iridescent shimmer, can be used

Working out regularly at the gym, writing in your journal or meditating can help you manage your stress.

on the brow and sacral chakra. It's readily available as natural and tumbled stones. Moonstone balances hormones, eases mood swings and stress, and enhances intuition.

Aqua aura, a clear quartz crystal bonded in the laboratory with gold vapour, produces an intense electric or sky-blue colour. It's

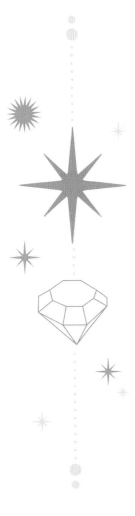

Keeping a
sleep diary can
also help you
become aware
of behaviour
patterns
that may be
disturbing
your sleep.

used on the crown, brow and throat chakra. Being a protective stone, aqua aura activates the upper chakras and helps safeguard you from pollution and from negative people and situations. It is particularly effective in strengthening the thymus gland, an important part of the immune system. Its alchemical bond with gold attracts prosperity and financial good fortune.

Green fluorite is a transparent or semi-transparent cube-shaped or octahedral crystal; sometimes fused into pairs, used on the heart chakra. Some types glow or become 'fluorescent' under ultraviolet light. This stone relieves heartburn, indigestion, stomach cramps and stress-related ailments. Paired fluorite crystals enhance partnerships and co-operation at home and at work.

Smoky quartz are long, pointed crystals or tumbled stones, from smoky brown to dark grey in colour.

Very dark quartz may have been artificially irradiated. They can be used on the root chakra, and help reduce anxiety and other negative emotions, and balances and restores the body's energy after a period of illness or depression. Use it to draw off emotional or physical pain, especially in the abdomen, hips and legs.

Being a protective stone, aqua aura activates the upper chakras and helps safeguard you from pollution and from negative people and situations.

CRYSTALS
FOR YOUR
EMOTIONS

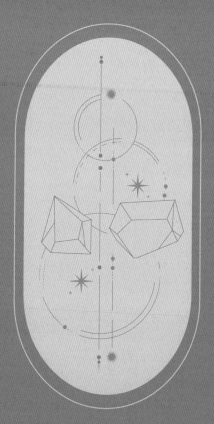

Because they work on the mind and body energetically, crystals are especially helpful in overcoming mental and emotional problems. From time to time the flow of life-force through the chakras can become unbalanced and emotional problems may indicate that either too much or too little energy is travelling through a chakra. Your own experience is likely to confirm this idea. Think of how constricted your heart feels when you are lonely or how much fiery energy you feel in your solar plexus when you are angry. Crystals help you to balance the flow of your energy and improve your mental and emotional health.

As you have learned, the seven chakras correspond to major areas of your life, including your psychological and emotional health. As the subtle electromagnetic vibration of a crystal resonates with the energy of a chakra, it helps to 'tune' the chakra's energy flow, drawing off excess energy or infusing additional energy as needed.

The first step in using crystals for emotional healing is to identify which chakra influences your problem.

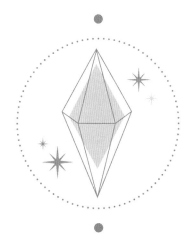

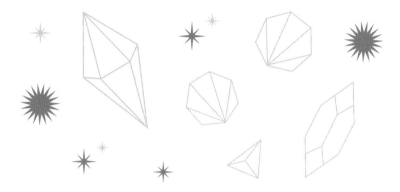

The root chakra influences emotional survival issues. Too little root chakra energy can make you excessively fearful or give you a tendency to feel ungrounded. Too much energy can manifest in clinging to possessions, people or excess body weight. Bloodstone is a great crystal that helps you to feel grounded, protected and secure.

The sacral chakra influences sexuality and emotional flow. Too little sacral chakra energy can make it difficult for you to feel emotional or sexual pleasure. Too much energy can make you feel as if you are swinging back and forth between emotional extremes. Orange calcite helps you to overcome sexual fears and balance your emotions of constantly needing the pleasurable stimulation of partners or sex.

The solar plexus chakra influences power and will. Too little of this energy can make you feel timid, tired or reluctant to take on power or responsibility. Too much, can manifest in needing always to be in control of others or to feeling constantly angry. Tiger's eye helps you to use your resources to accomplish your goals.

The sacral chakra influences sexuality and emotional flow.

The heart chakra influences love and relationships. Too little energy can make you feel self-centred, or fearful of intimacy. Too much energy can lead to a lack of appropriate emotional boundaries, or emotional neediness. Rose quartz can help in opening your heart to love, and in relieving heartache and grief.

The heart chakra influences love and relationships.

Too little throat chakra energy can make it difficult for you to speak up in groups or to express yourself clearly In writing.

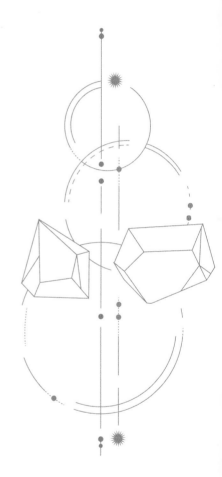

The throat chakra influences the spheres of communication and creative expression. Insufficient throat chakra energy can make it difficult for you to speak up in groups or to express yourself clearly in writing. However, too much can lead to talking too much or too loudly, often without saying anything very important. Aquamarine helps to clear blocked communication and promotes self-expression.

The brow chakra influences perception and intuition. Too little brow chakra energy can make it hard for you to see what's really going on around you or to trust your intuitive perceptions. Too much can cause you to have nightmares and difficulty separating reality from illusion. Lapis lazuli encourages clear thinking, self-awareness and vision.

The crown chakra influences knowledge and understanding. Not enough crown chakra energy can lead to rigid or narrow-minded thinking. Excessive energy can cause you to feel detached from the real world and to seem to be always living in your head. Apophyllite encourages introspection and supports truthful understanding.

RELAXATION AND STRESS RELIEF

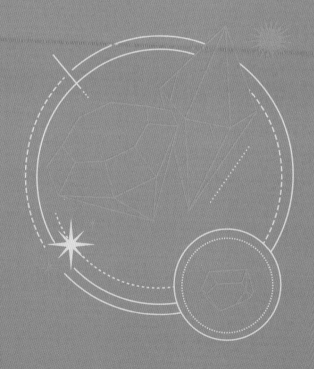

You've no doubt had days when everything seems to go wrong and your emotional reactions are way over the top. You may be so upset that you can't stop crying, or you may feel so worked up that you can barely think straight.

Physiologically, what's happening is that your adrenal glands are secreting a hormone that causes the 'on alert' feeling that is often called the 'fight or flight' response. When being on stress alert turns into a regular habit, your body's energy reserves become depleted. Over time, you may be at risk of stress-related ailments such as heart disease, high blood pressure, migraines and depression.

Crystals can provide an energetic aid to relaxation and stress relief. Because of their soothing and balancing effect on all levels of your being, they can help your body slow the release of stress hormones, increase your awareness of negative thought patterns and mental attitudes and quieten your emotional responses.

The crystals listed below are among the most useful for relieving stress and promoting relaxation:

- Amethyst relieves tension headaches brought on by stress.

- Bloodstone grounds your body and reduces irritability and impatience.

- Labradorite releases fears and insecurities and calms an overactive mind.

- Rose quartz soothes the emotions and helps to slow the release of stress hormones.

- Tiger's eye helps to reduce any self-criticism and negative thought patterns that may be contributing to stress.

CRYSTAL HEALING

This technique uses a pair of balancing crystals – one that draws out stressful energy and one that fills your body and mind with soothing vibrations. The first crystal listed in each pair below relieves stress. The second crystal calms and soothes.

Amber and Blue chalcedony: Amber absorbs negative energy, while blue chalcedony promotes acceptance and optimism.

Clear quartz and Amethyst: Clear quartz relieves pain and tension, while amethyst brings calmness and mental clarity.

1. Choose one of the crystal pairs above. Sit comfortably or lie on your back on a yoga mat or folded blanket.

2. Hold the more active crystal (the first crystal in each pair) in your dominant hand (the hand you write with) and hold the calming crystal in your receptive hand.

3. Close your eyes. Consciously relax your muscles, starting with your feet and working your way up your body. Allow about 20 minutes for the crystals to do their work.

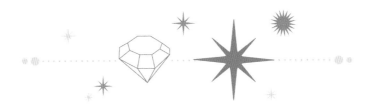

When you are anxious about something, you may feel as if your thoughts are no longer under your control. Persistent worry can negatively impact on your physical health as well as your emotional wellbeing. You may develop headaches and muscle pain, or you may have trouble sleeping.

Cultures around the world have used crystals to release the nervous tension that accompanies worry. Some of the most useful ones are listed below.

Kunzite, is a tranquil pink stone that has a mood-lifting effect. It helps to clear stuck emotional energy and to break the worry cycle of obsessive thoughts.

Lepidolite soothes emotional distress and helps overcome insomnia. This calming purple stone is also valuable in helping to release old thought patterns.

Feeling fearful when you are in actual danger is part of your body's natural self-protection mechanism. Feeling apprehensive before you give a speech or visit the dentist is also natural, so long as you are able to control your fear and keep going. But when fear interferes with your ability to enjoy life fully, it may be a reason for concern.

An intense, irrational fear of a situation or object is called a phobia. Common phobias include fear of closed-in places, heights, tunnels, lifts, water, flying and spiders! Phobias get in the way of daily living by redirecting your life energy towards avoiding the thing you fear. They can also cause physical symptoms, such as stomach cramps or light-headedness. Untreated, they can lead to addictions and social isolation.

RELEASING YOUR PHOBIAS

For this exercise you will need one aquamarine crystal with a single termination and/or one smoky quartz crystal with a single termination. Aquamarine brings courage and calms your mind. Smoky quartz helps keep your body grounded in fearful situations. Use either technique or one after the other, depending on your need.

Technique 1

1. Sit comfortably cross-legged on the floor or on a chair with feet flat on the floor. Place the crystals nearby. Close your eyes and follow your breathing all the way in and all the way out until you feel both centred and relaxed.

2. With the fingers of your right hand, tap your breastbone three times between your heart and your throat. This place is the witness point.

3. Hold the aquamarine to your witness point with the termination towards your head. Think about the fear or phobia you want to release. You may feel tingling or throbbing in your witness point as your mind becomes calm.

Technique 2

1. Follow steps 1 and 2 from Technique 1.

2. In Step 3, hold the smoky quartz to your witness point with the termination towards your lap (downwards). Think about the fear or phobia you want to release. You may feel tingling or throbbing in your witness point as your fear is released and body becomes more grounded and centred.

Anger feels awful. Your heart races and it hurts to breathe. Anger is often hot and raging. It can make you yell or throw things or pound your fist on the table. Hot rage can lead to aggression, but anger does not always look hot. It can also manifest as passive-aggressive behaviour and coldly calculated strategies to get back at someone who has hurt you.

The sacral chakra influences sexuality and emotional flow.

Ironically, anger often hurts you as much as it hurts the person towards whom it is directed. In Buddhism anger has been described as reaching your hand into the fire to pick up a hot coal to throw at someone else. Of course, your hand gets burned first!

Crystals can help you to release your angry feelings before they cause you damage.

Apophyllite calms and grounds your spirit, and helps you to clearly see the truth in anger-provoking situations.

Amethyst works like a natural tranquilizer to dispel anger and bring patience and acceptance.

Lapis lazuli opens the throat chakra, allowing you to express any repressed anger that may be blocking your ability to communicate.

Daily life provides many examples of the close connection between your emotions and your mental processes. On days when you are depressed or your self-confidence is low, your mind may feel sluggish or confused, or it may skip restlessly from one topic to another. It may be hard to focus and you may forget appointments or be unable to finish tasks and meet deadlines. Crystals can help to calm an overactive mind and clear confusion.

✳

Daily life provides many examples of the close connection between your emotions and your mental processes.

✳

LOVE AND RELATIONSHIPS

Crystals can help you enhance the energy of the two chakras most closely linked to love and relationships: the sacral chakra and the heart chakra. A well-functioning sacral chakra will connect you to your feelings and make it possible for you to enjoy physical pleasure. The heart chakra adds the bonds of love to your relationships.

A well-functioning sacral chakra will connect you to your feelings and make it possible for you to enjoy physical pleasure.

The sacral chakra governs sexuality. Blockages here can make it hard for you to feel desire. A well-functioning sacral chakra opens you to the joys of touching and being touched, of giving and receiving, of achieving sexual satisfaction and enjoying the sensation of giving satisfaction to others.

Orange-coloured crystals such as carnelian, orange calcite and citrine vibrate with the energy of the sacral chakra, releasing blockages and encouraging the free flow of sexual energy. Carnelian is especially effective for heightening interest in sex, overcoming impotence and strengthening the reproductive organs.

SACRAL PLEASURE

For this technique you will need one or two pieces of orange carnelian, orange calcite or citrine.

1. Prepare a private place to work in that's warm enough for you to be comfortable without clothes. If you wish, use candles, and soft music to make the space more intimate and relaxing.

2. Take off your clothes and lie down on a yoga mat or folded blanket. Place a flat pillow under your head to ease any tension in your neck.

3. Place the orange-coloured crystal on your sacral chakra, just below your navel.

4. As you breathe in, visualize the air coming in through your nose and travelling down your body, carrying warmth and energy to your lower abdomen. Visualize or feel a vibrant orange glow flowing from the crystal into your sacral chakra, awakening and healing your sexual centre. You should continue the visualization for 5–15 minutes.

HEALING WITH ROSE QUARTZ

This meditation will open you to all the possibilities of romance. You will need one polished rose quartz crystal carved into the shape of a heart.

1. Lie on your back on a yoga mat or blanket. Place a flat pillow under your head to ease any tension in your neck.

2. Place the rose quartz heart on your heart chakra, between your breasts.

3. Spend a few minutes watching your breath, paying attention to the expansion and contraction of your chest.

4. Bring to mind the image of someone you love or have loved strongly in your life. Appreciate as fully as you can everything that was or is wonderful about this relationship.

5. Now turn your attention to your heart chakra. Visualize it as a beautiful budding rose being warmed by the gentle vibrations of the rose quartz heart. Allow the tender feelings you have for the loved person you are recalling slowly to open the petals of the rosebud until your heart rose is in full and glorious bloom.

Rose quartz has a strong energetic connection to the heart chakra.

Rose quartz has a strong energetic connection to the heart chakra. Often called the stone of unconditional love, it encourages healthy self-love, forgiveness and reconciliation and opens the heart to romantic love. Rose quartz is also a comforting stone when you have suffered heartbreak, especially grief over the loss of someone you have loved.

Crystals can help you surround yourself with bubble of safety and protection at home.

If you have been hurt in your relationships, you may have closed down the flow of energy through your heart chakra to protect yourself from being hurt again. Opening to unhappy memories

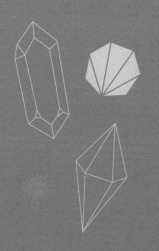

is sometimes painful, but it is a necessary first step to getting your emotional energy moving again.

Healthy emotional balance also depends on living in a safe and protected environment. Emotionally sensitive people are often prone to 'picking up' stress, anger and other negative emotions from the people around them. If you commute on public transport, for instance, you may absorb negative emotional energy fromliterally hundreds of strangers before you even get to work. Many people are also sensitive to the electromagnetic pollution generated by computers, mobile phones and other appliances. Crystals can help you surround yourself with bubble of safety and protection at home, at work and when you're on the go.

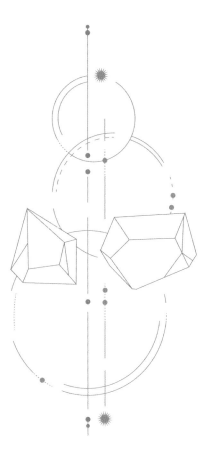

AT HOME

- Place an amethyst geode
  or large cluster near the
  front door of your home
  for general protection.

- Create a protective grid by
  placing crystals at each corner
  of your home. For a building, the
  crystals can be placed outside,
  at each exterior corner. Large
  chunky crystals of sodalite,
  smoky quartz, citrine, amber,
  kunzite, aragonite, carnelian,
  jasper, amethyst, labradorite,
  bloodstone, lapis lazuli and
  rose quartz are especially
  effective. If the crystal you
  have chosen has a point, aim
  it away from the house to
  deflect negative energy.

- Ensure serenity in your garden
  by decorating pots of flowers
  with citrine and tiger's eye
  instead of rocks.

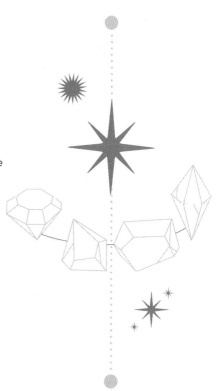

AT WORK

- Put a piece of fluorite or a quartz cluster on top of your computer to protect yourself from electromagnetic pollution.

- Position a clear quartz cluster on your desk to dispel static electricity.

- A large smoky quartz placed on your desk can protect you from picking up other people's stress and frustration.

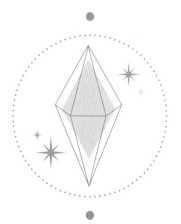

✳

If you have been hurt in your relationships, you may have closed down the flow of energy through your heart chakra to protect yourself from being hurt again.

✳

CRYSTALS TO BALANCE YOUR EMOTIONS

In this section, you'll find a directory of crystals for your emotions. They are arranged by colour, which, as your recall, loosely corresponds to the chakras from your crown to the root.

Apophyllite, are clear white cubic or pyramidal crystals, which may have a green, yellow or pink tint. They're available as small single crystals or larger clusters, and work well with the crown chakra.

Discovered at the start of the 19th century, this crystal's name derives from the Greek word apophylliso, meaning 'it flakes off', a reference to its tendency to flake apart when heated.

The high water content makes this stone an energy conductor. It aids mental clarity and memory, calms worry and fear, reduces stress and enhances spiritual vision.

Lepidolite are layered transparent or translucent shiny crystals, ranging in colour from purple to pink. They're easily obtained in natural and polished form, and are linked to the crown and brow chakra.

Discovered in the 18th century, the stone has a violet colour which comes from lithium, a mood stabilizer.

Lepidolite clears electromagnetic pollution generated by computers, absorbs stress and helps escape from behavioural patterns, including addictions. This stone also facilitates positive life changes, such as to a new house, partner or job.

> **Because of its resemblance to the starry night sky, lapis is considered to be a stone of serenity and peace.**

Lapis lazuli are deep blue, opaque crystals, often flecked with gold. Readily available in raw or tumbled form, these crystals are to be used on the brow and throat chakra.

Prized as a gemstone since 5000 BCE, lapis lazuli was sacred to the gods and pharaohs of ancient Egypt, as can be seen by its frequent use in jewellery and other treasures found in Egyptian tombs.

Because of its resemblance to the starry night sky, lapis is considered to be a stone of serenity and peace. It encourages clarity and self-awareness and supports clear communication, especially the expression of emotions.

Aquamarine is a clear, sometimes watery-looking crystal, ranging in colour from light blue to blue-green. It's readily available in natural and tumbled form, and is paired with the throat chakra.

Latin for 'water of the sea', aquamarine is called the sailor's

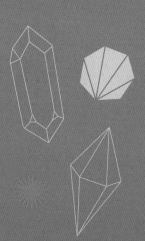

Lepidolite clears electromagnetic pollution generated by computers.

stone because sailors used it as an amulet to protect themselves from storms and seasickness. In myth, it is sacred to Aphrodite, the goddess born from sea foam, and other ancient sea goddesses and mermaids.

This calming stone brings courage and relieves fears and phobias, especially those connected to travel. It also clears blockages to self-expression and helps overcome negative thinking and the feeling of being overwhelmed by responsibility.

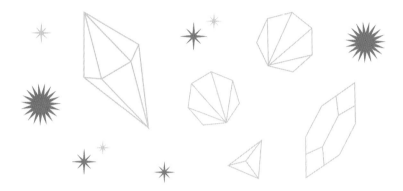

Rose quartz is a translucent pink stone, linked to the heart chakra. It's easily obtained in natural and polished form, often carved into spheres, wands and hearts.

In myth, Adonis, the mortal lover of the goddess Aphrodite, was gored by a boar. Rushing to save him, Aphrodite was caught on a thorn bush. The lovers' mingled blood stained the white quartz pink, making this stone a symbol of love since Roman times.

The most important crystal for the heart chakra, calm and peaceful rose quartz opens the heart to love. It is called the crystal of reconciliation because it encourages empathy and forgiveness, releases unexpressed emotions and soothes grief and heartache.

Kunzite, are semi-transparent flat or striated crystals, pink to lilac in colour. Newly discovered deposits are making this rare stone more widely available, and are to be used on the heart chakra.

Discovered in California in 1903, this beautiful gem-quality stone was named in honour of New York jeweller and gemstone specialist Dr George Frederic Kunz, who first described it.

A peaceful, loving stone with particular affinity to womxn, kunzite helps dissolve negativity and heal emotional instability. It builds confidence and is effective in relieving panic attacks and depression from emotional causes. Worn as jewellery, it protects against environmental stress and the negative feelings of others.

The most important crystal for the heart chakra, calm and peaceful rose quartz opens the heart to love.

In China, amber is said to be petrified dragon's blood or to contain the power of many suns.

Amber is an organic gemstone, actually the fossilized resin of trees that grew 30 million years ago. Translucent yellow or golden orange, sometimes containing fossilized insects or plants. It's easily obtained, and used on the solar plexus chakra.

In China, amber is said to be petrified dragon's blood or to contain the power of many suns. The Vikings called it the tears of their love goddess, Freya. Amber has been used throughout history as a protective amulet.

A powerful cleanser and healer, this crystal absorbs all kinds of emotional distress as well as promoting warm, bright and sunny optimism. It also increases a sense of self-worth and attracts prosperity.

Tiger's eye is a yellow crystal with a silky lustre and golden-brown or honey-coloured bands, and is easily obtained in natural form or as small tumbled stones.

This stone is directly linked to the solar plexus chakra.

So named because it resembles the eye of a tiger, this attractive stone also imparts a tiger's fearlessness and Roman soldiers frequently carried it for courage and protection in battle.

As a grounding stone, tiger's eye combines stable Earth energy with the energetic power of the sun. It promotes integrity, the proper use of power and finishing what you start. It balances the emotions, calms scattered thinking and helps to resolve dilemmas and internal conflicts.

Tiger's eye combines stable Earth energy with the energetic power of the sun.

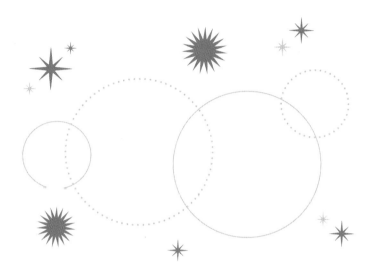

Labradorite are grey to black stones with iridescent blue or gold flashes, and are readily available as small to large tumbled stones. They are used on the solar plexus chakra.

The name comes from the Labrador peninsula of Canada, where the stone was discovered. In Eskimo lore, it is said to contain the trapped brilliance of the Northern Lights. In Finland, it was often used by shamans in ritual work.

A powerful protector, labradorite deflects negative thoughts and unwanted energy and banishes insecurity and fear. It calms an overactive mind, dispels illusions and balances rational thinking with intuition. Emotionally, it supports self-trust and stability in times of transition.

Aragonite, in its natural form, often grows as twin crystals or as branching tree or coral-like clusters. This orange to brown crystal can be easily obtained, and is linked to the sacral chakra.

Discovered in Aragon, Spain, from where it draws its name, this crystal provides the pearly, iridescent colours in the shells of abalone and other sea creatures. It is also found in hot springs, volcanic rocks and caves.

A powerful Earth healer, this stone keeps you centred and grounded and teaches you to think before you act. It combats anger and bad temper, encourages patience, practicality and responsibility, and provides strength and support at times of emotional distress.

A powerful protector, labradorite deflects negative thoughts and unwanted energy and banishes insecurity and fear.

Excellent for stimulating sexual energies, orange calcite also promotes creativity.

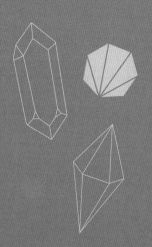

Calcite are translucent, waxy orange to peach-coloured crystals, often banded with darker orange. It's readily available in natural or tumbled form, used on the sacral chakra.

The name comes from the Greek word chalix, which means 'lime'. One of the most common minerals on Earth, calcite is the primary component of cave formations such as stalactites, stalagmites and veils.

Excellent for stimulating sexual energies, orange calcite also promotes creativity. It relieves depression, combats fear and phobias and restores emotional equilibrium.

Bloodstone, also known as heliotrope, is a handsome stone that's dark green flecked with red or orange. It's used on the root and sacral chakra, readily available in tumbled form.

According to Christian myth, when Christ was crucified, his blood fell on a green stone at his feet, which became known as bloodstone. In medieval Europe, the stone was thought to stop bleeding and as a result was often carried by soldiers.

An excellent grounding and protective stone, bloodstone imparts courage and helps you defend yourself against physical and emotional dangers. It brings good luck, anchors you in the present moment and revitalizes you when you are exhausted.

Bloodstone, also known as heliotrope, is a handsome stone.

CRYSTALS
FOR SPIRITUAL
HARMONY

Because of their unique ability to focus and transmit psychic energy, crystals can strengthen your natural spiritual abilities. A crystal's spiritual power is enhanced by your motivation and intention. If you seek inner balance, crystals can help you align your body's energies. If you wish to create harmony in your environment, crystals can make your home a peaceful sanctuary. Holding a crystal during meditation helps you sharpen your intuition, enlarge your creative vision and deepen your ability to concentrate. Placed under your pillow with intention, crystals can open you to dreams that provide spiritual guidance and personal insight.

Crystals have been valued since ancient times as aids to vision, intuition, wisdom and other psychic and spiritual gifts. As you will discover in this chapter, working with crystals can help you develop these qualities in yourself.

Everyone has natural psychic gifts. You've probably experienced times when a hunch told you what would happen, when you 'just knew' what you had to do, or when a dream gave you insight into a current situation. Crystals do not provide these intuitive abilities; rather, they help you develop and strengthen the skills you already have.

Crystal gazing, or scrying, is the ancient practice of seeking visions by gazing into a reflective surface, such as a crystal ball, a mirror or a pool of water. The crystal ball does not produce the images – they are produced by the mind and projected onto the crystal ball, which acts like a screen.

The real picture-making magic is in your mind. It is the same ability that allows you to 'see' an apple in your mind's eye when you hear the word.

As you have learned, the ability to envision and to visualize is influenced by the brow chakra, which also controls intuition and psychic gifts such as clairvoyance, the ability to 'see' future events or to receive information from a distant location, and telepathy, the ability to communicate with another mind. You'll have the opportunity to use crystals to develop and strengthen these natural psychic gifts later in this chapter.

The natural beauty of crystals can enhance the decor of your home or office.

Crystals can also help you strengthen your ability to meditate. Meditation allows you to turn your consciousness inwards and enter a peaceful state of relaxed awareness in which your mind can more easily connect with the divine energies of universal mind. Crystals that open and stimulate the crown chakra – your gateway to spiritual connection – can facilitate this process.

Crystals can also help you focus your intention on your dreams and use them to seek advice and guidance for your life. By stimulating the throat and brow chakras, they encourage vivid dreams and help you use your intuition to decode a dream's symbols and understand its messages.

You can also use crystals to balance your internal energies and to harmonize the energies in your surroundings. Placed on your chakras with intention, crystals can help you clear blockages in your energy pathways and bring your internal energies into harmonious alignment. Similarly, you can harmonize the energies in your home or office by using your intuition to place appropriate crystals in various locations.

The natural beauty of crystals can enhance the decor of your home or office. Sited with intention, crystals can also harmonize the energy of your environment to suit your activities and match your moods.

Crystals intended for display are generally larger than the crystals you use for personal healing. Large raw crystals, crystal clusters and beautiful geodes, spheres and pillars are especially suitable.

Meditation allows you to turn your consciousness inwards and enter a peaceful state of relaxed awareness.

CRYSTAL PLACEMENT

Here are some suggestions for where to place your crystals. However, your own intuition is always your best guide.

Citrine energizes and recharges you, as well as encouraging an attitude of abundance and optimism.

Pay attention to how you feel over a period of several days after putting a crystal in place. Often the crystal itself will 'tell' you – by stimulating your intuition – whether the site is appropriate.

Here are some suggestions for where to place your crystals. However, your own intuition is always your best guide.

Pay attention to how you feel over a period of several days after putting a crystal in place. Often the crystal itself will 'tell' you – by stimulating your intuition – whether the site is appropriate.

BATHROOM

Watery crystals like blue lace agate, aquamarine, moonstone, selenite and pink and watermelon tourmaline are perfect for placing in the bathroom.

Pay attention to how you feel over a period of several days after putting a crystal in place.

Try putting a few polished blue lace agate or aquamarine crystals into your bathwater. As you soak in the bath, allow the crystal energies to relax and soothe your emotions and prompt your intuition to provide insights into issues that may be troubling you.

LIVING ROOM/LOUNGE

Citrine energizes and recharges you, as well as encouraging an attitude of abundance and optimism. Place a citrine cluster or geode in the corner of the room farthest to the back and to the left of the entry door (the 'wealth corner' according to the Chinese art of placement) to support your wish for a happy, successful and prosperous life.

KITCHEN

Since the kitchen is often the heart of the home, green-coloured crystals such as green fluorite, green aventurine and jade can enhance its loving and nourishing warmth. Place a selection of green crystals on your kitchen windowsill or use a green marble bowl filled with fruit or vegetables as a kitchen table centrepiece.

BEDROOM

You have already learned that rose quartz is the ideal crystal for encouraging positive love relationships. Other appropriate crystals for placing in the bedroom include green aventurine, which promotes empathy and stress-free relationships, pink tourmaline, a crystal aphrodisiac that encourages sexual pleasure, and red jasper, which aids dream recall when placed under your pillow.

OFFICE OR HOME OFFICE

Crystals that combine the colours red and green, such as bloodstone and watermelon tourmaline, are ideal for placing in your workspace.

Watermelon tourmaline helps you to understand situations and act with patience, diplomacy and tact. Bloodstone encourages clarity and reduces irritation, aggressive attitudes and impatience.

If you could see your chakras, as some energy healers do, each one would appear as a rotating wheel of coloured light, perhaps 7–12 cm (3–5 inches) in diameter. When your body, your emotions and your spiritual nature are all in harmonious balance, your chakras are aligned vertically and all are about the same size. Each chakra also displays its own clear and characteristic colour.

Though you may not be able to see your chakras with your physical eyes, you can use your intuition to sense them.

FULL CHAKRA CLEANSE

You can also use crystals to cleanse and balance all of your chakras at once. Feel free to substitute other crystals of the appropriate colours that feel intuitively right to you.

Gather the following crystals or others of your own choosing:

- one tumbled smoky quartz (below your feet)

- one tumbled red jasper (root chakra)

- one tumbled fire opal (sacral chakra)

- one tumbled sunstone (solar plexus chakra)

- one tumbled green aventurine (heart chakra)

- one tumbled turquoise (throat chakra)

- one tumbled azurite with malachite (brow chakra)

- one tumbled amethyst (crown chakra)

- one tumbled clear quartz (above your head)

1. Lie down on a yoga mat or folded blanket. Place a flat pillow under your head to ease tension in your neck.

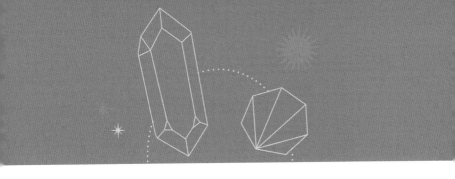

2. Before you put the crystals in place, consider for a few moments your motivation for engaging in this process. For instance, remind yourself that you are more than just your physical body and your consciousness.

3. As you place the crystals as indicated previously, starting with the smoky quartz below your feet, remind yourself that the light and energy of each crystal is working in harmony with the energy of your own chakras.

4. Leave the crystals in place for at least 20 minutes. Remain relaxed and alert. Focus your attention on each chakra in turn, starting with your root chakra and working your way up to the crown. Feel that the energy of the crystal is clearing blockages in your energy pathways and regulating the chakra's size and spin.

5. When you feel ready, gather up the crystals, starting with the clear quartz above your head and working downwards to the smoky quartz below your feet. Gently roll to one side and stand up slowly, feeling that your feet are firmly on the ground and that your life energy is harmonious and balanced.

CHAKRA COLOUR BALANCE

If you sense a variation in the size, or colour of one of your chakras – for instance, a throat chakra that is pale rather than vivid blue, or a solar plexus chakra that has too little energy or seems to be spinning too slowly – use the colour balancing technique below to strengthen the chakra's energy.

Crystals that vibrate at a similar colour frequency can help to regulate the chakra's spin and bring it back into alignment.

1. Consult the chakra list on pages 22-25 and choose a crystal that corresponds in colour to the chakra that you wish to strengthen.

2. Sit comfortably cross-legged on the floor or on a chair with your feet flat on the floor. Be sure that your back is straight. Breathe gently and smoothly in a regular rhythm.

3. Hold the crystal you have chosen in your hands. Visualize the coloured light and energy of the crystal radiating out and flowing into your chakra, balancing and strengthening its energy. Maintain a state of relaxed awareness for 5–10 minutes.

There's nothing magical about intuition. The human mind is amazingly complex.

There's nothing magical about intuition. The human mind is amazingly complex. In addition to dealing with the day-to-day information from your senses, your thinking processes and your emotions, it also encodes memories, fantasies and unconscious thoughts and feelings. Some psychologists estimate that 95 per cent of the contents of the mind are unconscious and beneath the surface of everyday awareness, like an iceberg with its great bulk hidden under the water.

The 'voices' that you hear and the 'visions' that you see when you go inside to access your intuition are, in fact, part of you. They reflect the understanding you have gained everything from what you have experienced in your life – even things you have forgotten or never consciously knew.

Quietening your everyday mind creates the space for the deep wisdom of your mind to provide inspiration and guidance. Using a crystal sphere as a focus point is a time-honoured method of accessing this wisdom.

CRYSTAL GAZING

For this exercise you will need a sphere of clear quartz, obsidian or smoky quartz and a small white candle.

1. Light the candle and dim the lights in the room. Hold the crystal sphere in your cupped hands for several moments and focus on your breathing, continuing until you feel relaxed and centred.

2. As you hold the sphere, clarify your intention. Phrase what you wish to know in a clear, and positive way.

3. Place the sphere in front of you with the burning candle behind it.

4. Gaze at the crystal with half-closed eyes and allow images to form in your mind and on the sphere.

5. When you feel that the process is complete, acknowledge what you have discovered as the deep wisdom of your own intuition. Wrap the crystal sphere in a cloth and blow out the candle.

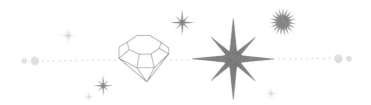

With practice and good intentions, anyone can develop psychic gifts such as clairvoyance and telepathy to some degree. Used with integrity and the proper motivation, these gifts can help you extend your mind and senses beyond the horizons of time and space and discover information that is helpful for you and others.

With practice and good intentions, anyone can develop psychic gifts such as clairvoyance and telepathy.

One of the most powerful crystals for developing your psychic gifts is moldavite. This strange crystal is said to be of extra-terrestrial origin. It was formed about 15 million years ago when a meteor collided with Earth in the Moldau river valley in the Czech Republic. Combining the energies of Earth and the heavens, moldavite encourages psychic and spiritual growth.

Moldavite can help you journey forwards into the future or backwards into the past. You might journey into your own future to gain insight into the consequences of your current actions or you might journey backwards in time to gain insight into the lives of your grandparents or other ancestors.

Many people misunderstand the goal of meditation. Meditation is not a passive activity, and although relaxing your body and calming your mind are among its benefits, they are not its central purpose. The aim of meditation is focused awareness – a state of being more present to yourself.

One useful way to think about meditation is as a form of clear internal communication. As you quiet your body and mind and look inside yourself, you become aware that your perceptions, emotions, thoughts and beliefs, including beliefs about yourself

The aim of meditation is focused awareness – a state of being more present to yourself.

such as 'I have a bad temper' or 'I can't manage money', are not permanent and unchanging. Instead, they come and go, like clouds passing across the sky. Crystals can also help this process.

BLUE SKY MEDITATION

For this exercise you will need one blue-coloured crystal, such as a piece of lapis lazuli.

1. Sit comfortably on a cushion or a chair with your feet flat on the floor. Hold the crystal to your throat for a few moments. Imagine that you are inhaling the bright blue energy of the crystal, relaxing your throat and enhancing your ability to communicate truthfully with yourself. Then relax and hold the crystal gently in your lap.

2. Bring to awareness whatever thoughts or emotions are passing through your mind at this moment. Do not follow these thoughts or feelings. Simply observe them.

3. All the thoughts and feelings that pass through your mind are like clouds that move across the sky, coming into view and then passing away. Remind yourself that these passing clouds are not your mind. Your mind is like the sky – vast, clear, empty and filled with light.

4. Focus on the clear blue sky of mind beyond all thoughts and feelings for 10–20 minutes, or until you feel relaxed, aware and at peace.

Meditation is also an opportunity to connect with the spiritual realm. Crystals with a high vibration, such as selenite, angelite and celestite, stimulate the higher chakras, lifting you to an awareness of universal consciousness – the realm in which you are simultaneously uniquely yourself and yet one with everything that is.

Connecting with this level of being regularly has the power to transform your life. You realize that you are much more than your physical body and your mind. Like a crystal, you are essentially light energy that has been slowed down or frozen into physical form. Meditation gives your inner light a chance to shine.

INNER LIGHT MEDITATION

You will need one piece of angelite, celestite or selenite.

1. Sit comfortably cross-legged on the floor or on a chair with your feet flat on the floor. Allow your eyes to close and take a few conscious breaths, following your breathing all the way in and all the way out.

2. Hold the crystal you have chosen above the top of your head for a few moments. Then relax and hold it gently in your lap.

3. Visualize that the crystal you held above your head has left behind a sphere of pure transparent white light. Spend a few moments focusing on the presence of this light. Don't worry if the sphere does not appear clearly. It's fine just to have a sense that it is there.

4. Imagine that this sphere of light represents every wonderful quality that you have ever wished for: compassion, generosity, patience, enthusiasm, wisdom – the complete fulfilment of your highest potential.

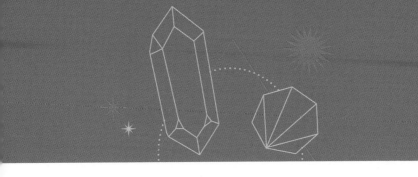

5. Imagine now that the sphere of light decreases in size, shrinking until it becomes the size of a bird's egg. Imagine that this sphere enters your body through your crown chakra and descends to your heart chakra, bringing these qualities into your heart.

6. Imagine now the sphere of light expands once more, slowly filling your entire body. As it does, feel that your physical parts, your perceptions, emotions, thoughts and beliefs are dissolving into light, becoming what they are in essence – pure formless energy.

7. Remain in this serene and joyful state as long as you wish.

CRYSTAL DREAMING

Grounding stones such as red jasper and bloodstone stimulate dreaming. Crystals with a higher vibration, can help you recall and decode dream messages.

For this exercise you will need one piece of red jasper or bloodstone and one piece of amethyst, danburite, celestite, or moonstone.

1. Before you go to sleep, place the bloodstone or red jasper under your pillow. Place a notebook and pen near your bed. Allow your last thought before falling asleep to be your intention to dream vividly and to remember your dreams.

2. When you awake, lie still and bring your dreams to mind. Write notes about everything you remember.

3. Later, set aside time to decode your dreams. Place your notebook in your lap and hold the amethyst, danburite or moonstone in your hands. Close your eyes and breathe in the energy of the crystal until you feel centred and relaxed.

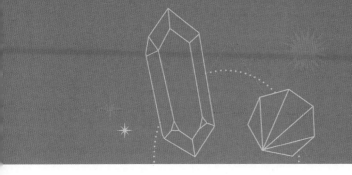

4. Begin by making associations. Assume that every person, place, colour, sound, situation and event in your dream is trying to tell you something. Write down every association you can for each image. An association is any feeling, word, memory or idea that pops up in response to an image.

5. Next, make personal connections. Look over your list of associations and decide which associations 'click' – that is, which spontaneously bring up energy or strong feeling. For each, ask yourself: What part of me is that? What do I have in common with that? Where have I seen that in my life? Make notes about what you discover.

6. Finally, find the message. Use your intuition to draw the associations and connections together into a unified picture. Ask yourself: What message is this dream trying to communicate? What changes is it advising me to make? Don't expect the message to be clear immediately. You'll know you are on the right track when an interpretation gives you a surge of energy.

The aim of meditation is focused
awareness – a state of being more
present to yourself.

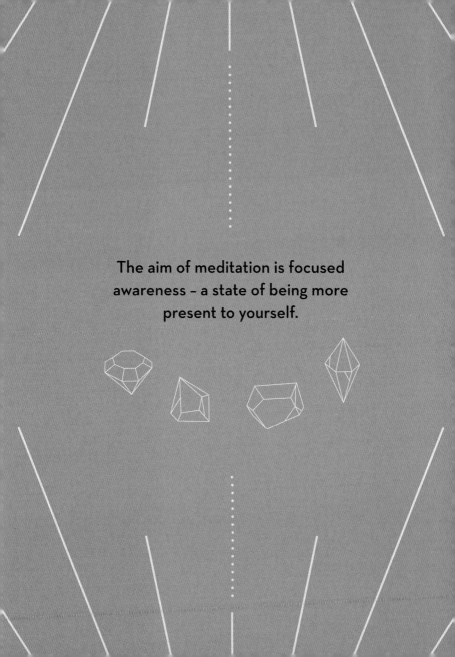

CRYSTALS FOR YOUR SPIRIT

In this section, you'll find a directory of crystals for your spirit.

Selenite is white, transparent or semi-transparent. The form called satin spar has fine white bands that look like satin. Easily obtained, and used on the crown chakra

Named for the moon goddess Selene, selenite symbolizes both change and predictability.

Selenite enhances meditation and psychic communication, including telepathy and clairvoyance, and promotes dream recall. Selenite pillars can be used for crystal gazing, especially for journeys to the past and future.

Moldavite is transparent and deep green, often blackish until held up to light. It's quite rare, but can be readily available – this is linked to the crown and brow chakra.

The properties of this spiritual stone relate to its extra-terrestrial origin. It has been used as a good luck and fertility talisman since prehistoric times.

Moldavite's high vibration opens and aligns the chakras and helps clear blockages in the energy pathways. Sometimes called the 'Grail stone', it can take you to the highest spiritual dimension, facilitate spiritual vision and out-of-body journeys.

Celestite is a wonderful meditation stone. It supports enhanced states of awareness and encourages a feeling of peace and unity.

Celestite is semi-transparent, pale or sky blue with white. Sometimes, it looks like ice crystals. Used on the crown, brow and throat chakra, this is easily obtained, but may be expensive.

The name 'celestite' means 'of the sky'. Popular lore says that the stone came from the star group called the Pleiades and that it encodes ancient celestial wisdom. It was first found in Italy in the 18th century.

Celestite is a wonderful meditation stone. It supports enhanced states of awareness and encourages a feeling of peace and unity. This crystal also enhances personal creative and artistic expression, peaceful negotiation, clairvoyant communication and dream recall.

Angelite can be opaque pale blue to blue-violet, with white and sometimes red specks. Its veins often look like wings, and it's used on the crown, brow and throat chakra.

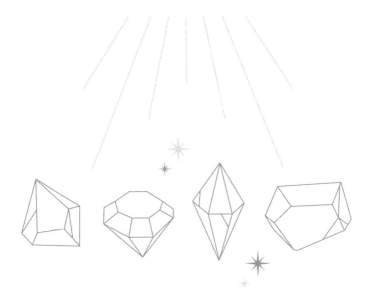

Formed from celestite that has been compressed for millions of years, angelite is considered to be the wiser stone of the two. First discovered in Peru, it was used as a healing crystal by indigenous Peruvian peoples.

Called a 'stone of awareness', angelite enhances perception, understanding and telepathic communication between minds and with spiritual beings. It supports creative self-expression, truth-telling and compassionate problem-solving. It also facilitates inspiration and creates a feeling of peace and tranquillity.

Azurite with **Malachite** is used on the brow chakra, and is a bright marbled blue and green stone, often with large green flecks and deep azure blue patches. Easily obtained.

For thousands of years this attractive combination stone has been used to make jewellery and ornamental objects. During the Middle Ages and Renaissance, it was ground into pigment for use in paint and cosmetics.

Like all combination stones, this crystal is more powerful than azurite or malachite alone. It opens the brow chakra to strengthen your ability to visualize and enhances spiritual vision. It is also an excellent meditation stone that aids psychic and spiritual healing.

Turquoise is an opaque light blue and blue green stone, often with darker veins. Used on the throat chakra, it can be easily obtained.

This stone's history dates back to ancient Egypt, where it was sacred to the goddess Hathor. It was also sacred to many Native American peoples, including the Pueblos, Apaches and Navajos, who used turquoise beads and carvings as protective and healing talismans.

This protective and stabilizing stone enhances intuition and communication. It is traditionally believed to unite Earth and sky, to harmonize masculine and feminine energies and to balance and align the chakras. As a meditation aid, it brings inner calm.

✳

Turquoise is an opaque light blue and blue green stone, often with darker veins.

✳

Watermelon tourmaline activates the heart chakra to enhance love, tenderness, patience and emotional healing.

Tourmaline is shiny, opaque or transparent – often with long striations, has many colours, including pink and pink enfolded or banded with green (watermelon tourmaline). This crystal is used on the heart chakra.

The last Empress of China, Tz'u Hsi, loved pink tourmaline and imported it to China from a mine in California. She was buried on a carved tourmaline pillow. Watermelon tourmaline was first discovered and mined in the 19th century in Maine, USA.

This stone aids self-love, relaxation and inner peace. As an aphrodisiac, it helps to harmonize sexuality and spirituality. Watermelon tourmaline activates the heart chakra to enhance love, tenderness, patience and emotional healing.

Green Aventurine is opaque, ranging from light to darker green, and often speckled with metallic

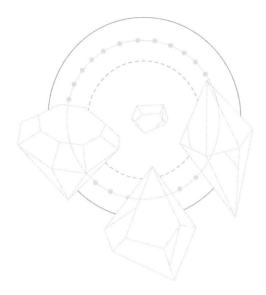

gold or silvery particles. Used on the heart chakra, this crystal is readily available.

The name comes from the Italian phrase a ventura, which means 'by chance'. Said to bring prosperity and good fortune, green aventurine is often called the 'gambler's stone' because it attracts money and has been found to be lucky in games of chance.

This protective stone heightens perception and stabilizes the mind. It stimulates creativity and optimism and helps you to see alternative possibilities. Placed over the heart chakra, it fosters tranquillity and opens the heart to compassion and spiritual growth.

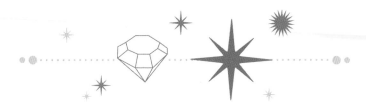

Sunstone is transparent or opaque, ranging in colour from gentle orange to vivid tangerine with golden iridescent flashes. Used on the solar plexus, this crystal is readily available.

This ancient gem, said to contain the power of the sun, was believed by the Vikings to be an aid to navigation and has been found in Viking burial mounds.

This joyful stone clears the chakras and brings in healing light and energy. It lifts dark moods and depression and attracts good fortune. It heightens intuition and facilitates self-empowerment and emotional independence. When used during meditation, it brings in the regenerative power of the sun.

Fire Opal, usually translucent, is milky with dark orange. Linked with the sacral chakra, it can have fiery streaks. This is very easily obtained.

Natural healers use fire opal to stimulate the body's energy pathways.

Natural healers use fire opal to stimulate the body's energy pathways. Related to the sun and to flashes of lightning, it is used as a talisman against forest fires and volcanic eruptions. It is also said to attract good luck in business.

This protective gem brings joy and enhances personal power and sexual energy. It facilitates life changes and offers support in times of emotional distress. A symbol of regeneration and hope, fire opal helps you to let go of the past and release your pent-up emotions.

CONCLUSION

Within this book, we have explored how crystals can be used to amplify and balance the flow of energy in your body and our surroundings. Using them is not a substitute for traditional medical care, and it's important to take this away with you when you begin to practice with crystals, as following these exercises daily can only take you so far in physical strength. That being said, healing with crystals can empower you to take personal responsibility for your health, using simple and natural methods.

From preparing a gem essence to add to your evening bathwater, to taking the time to pay attention to the messages your body is communicating with you, using crystals can enhance your natural spiritual abilities. They can create harmony in your home, at your office and in your relationships too.

Used together with the practice of meditation and mindfulness, you can allow your consciousness to enter a peaceful state, which is what we all need sometimes, especially when most of us are hastily running through life to fulfil all our goals.

So start small, with a few tumbled crystals. Get comfortable with the exercises, and believe in yourself and the spiritual journey you are about to embark on.